Explaining
Prophecy

Alex Buchanan

Sovereign World

Scripture quotations are from the New American Standard Version
of the Bible. Copyright © The Lockman Foundation
1960, 1962, 1963, 1968, 1975, 1977.

ISBN: 1-85240-075-7

SOVEREIGN WORLD LIMITED
P.O. Box 777, Tonbridge, Kent TN11 9XT, England.

Typeset and printed in the UK by Sussex Litho Ltd, Chichester, West Sussex.

Contents

Introduction

Prophecy is an important subject for Christians to study today because there is so much deception about, both in the world and the Church. Prophecy, together with the other gifts which often come with it, such as the word of wisdom and the word of knowledge, are part of God's defence against deception. When someone speaks out a true prophecy it shows a situation or someone's life as it really is. 1 Corinthians 14:24–25 shows this to be true. *'...if an unbeliever...enters, he is convicted by all, he is called to account by all; the secrets of his heart are disclosed; and so he will fall on his face and worship God, declaring that God is certainly among you.'* No one can hide things in their heart when this gift of God is spoken out, especially when the word of knowledge comes with it. A Christian man came to me for help saying, 'I keep doubting whether I am really saved, can you help me?' After praying with him, God helped me to prophesy and I said, 'You have never repented of that murder attempt on your brother 13 years ago; if you go to him and confess your sin, God will forgive you, and you will not doubt anymore.' He did so, and is now a minister in the church.

Satan is a liar, and he is trying to confuse the Church in many ways. He causes people to say things which are nearly all true, but there is a lie hidden away in their words which can do enormous damage if it is not uncovered. Prophecy will uncover this, and will save us from deception.

Therefore, we must not despise this Gift from God. He warns us not to do so in 1 Thessalonians 5:20. But we must not accept prophecy without examining it carefully. The Bible says that we must examine it carefully and pass judgement on it (1 Corinthians 14). We do this by first listening to it, then we must discuss it until we are sure that it came from God. Then the leaders must tell the people what they feel about it. I have written more about this in chapter 5.

I hope this book will help God's people to understand the gift of Prophecy, and to value it, and to learn to prophesy in the power of the Spirit.

Alex Buchanan
York 1991.

1

What Is Prophecy?

Prophecy is a gift from the Lord Jesus to His people, given through the Holy Spirit. When Christians ask Him to give them this gift, and if they keep asking until He does so, then they are able to speak out to others words which they did not prepare beforehand. These words will encourage and strengthen the Church, and in some cases will tell them what to do.

God speaks to His people in many ways, for instance; through preaching, Bible reading, visions, dreams, and even natural disasters such as drought and earthquakes. Visions or dreams are usually given to God's people, but they are occasionally given to heathen people including kings, as I describe below. God is not restricted to just one method of speaking to people. When you look at creation with all its varied aspects, it is hardly likely that such a God would choose only one way of sharing His feelings and plans to men and women.

However, my main subject is the way in which God speaks to us directly through prophecy. He loves to share His heart with us, and in a true prophecy we will hear what is in the heart and mind of God. He has always communicated with mankind, either through dreams, or angel messengers, or Scripture, but we are considering in this book how He speaks through prophecy by the power of the Holy Spirit. *'for no prophecy was ever made by an act of human will, but men moved by the Holy Spirit spoke from God'* (2 Peter 1:21).

God gives prophecy for the following reasons

1. To enable men to write Scripture
This was only given to a few men who wrote the Bible which we have today. Inspired words were given to these men by the Spirit, to enable them to write it (2 Peter 1:21). No one is able to prophesy or write in this way today.

2. To reveal His heart and mind to His people
At its highest level, prophecy comes through someone who understands the heart and mind of God, and then reveals it to us (Amos 3:7). But there are different levels of prophecy, simply because people vary in their spirituality, and their capacity to express things clearly. Someone in a church prophesied in these words, 'My children, I am with you.' This was a true prophetic word, and it brought a little comfort to some who heard it. However it was not as deep, life changing, and encouraging as another prophecy in which God showed a church what its real condition was, what they were to do about it, and in which God offered them the help of the Holy Spirit. The person who brought the first word was a godly woman, but the one who brought the second word was a man who prayed all the time, meditated in the Bible constantly, and who lived a life far cleaner than most.

Those who are constantly reading, studying and meditating on the Scriptures, and living holy lives are more likely to speak out strong clear prophecies than those who do not take so much trouble.

3. To show God's people some things which will happen in the future
Many years ago a godly man in Armenia warned people to move away because of trouble which would come to them if they stayed where they were. In another country Christians who were being persecuted were often warned through

prophecy that the police were on their way to arrest them, and they were able to escape.

The whole Book of Revelation is one long prophecy, including foretelling and forthtelling; ie, predicting the future, and declaring the current word of God (Rhema).

4. To give prophetic guidance to individual people or churches

Prophecy gives particular instructions about special needs which the Bible does not give. David Pawson writes, 'prophecy adds the "particular" to the "general" guidance of Scripture. The Bible gave strategy, prophecy provided tactics. God's past promises assured victory, but the when and where had to be "enquired of the Lord" by consulting prophets (2 Chronicles 18:6; 19:2; 20:20). The Bible tells us how to live, but not where; how to marry, but not who; how to do our job, but not what job. The *"sons of God"* are those who are *"led by the Spirit"* (Romans 8:14), as well as those who live by the Scripture.'

Prophecy includes visions and dreams, and angelic messages

The difference between a vision and a dream, is that a vision is seen while awake or conscious, and a dream is a vision seen whilst asleep or unconscious.

The Bible knows nothing about 'pictures'. When people in churches say that they have a picture, we must check it very carefully, for it could be something out of their own imagination. These mental concepts can be made to mean almost anything. In some cases though, people call something a picture when it is really a vision. They do this because they are afraid of seeming to be superspiritual if they use the term vision; but why be afraid when they only have to submit it to the church leadership and let them decide what is right or wrong in it?

Visions

God said that he would use these methods of communication. In the book of Numbers 12:6 God says, *'Hear now My words: if there is a prophet among you, I the Lord shall make Myself known to him in a vision. I shall speak with him in a dream.'*

God also said that visions and dreams would increase in the last days. Acts 2:17 says:

> *and it shall be in the last days... that I will pour forth of My Spirit upon all mankind; and your sons and your daughters shall prophesy, and your young men shall see visions, and your old men shall dream dreams.*

I believe that we are very close to these last days, therefore we should be asking for, and expecting these gifts to increase in our churches.

Ezekiel 8:3. God gave Ezekiel a vision of the idolatry going on in the very House of God. Secret sin in the Church is being exposed today through visions. God shows through them what otherwise would never be revealed. He does it because He longs for and demands, a pure Church.

Daniel 1:17. God gave Daniel and his friends visions, and these impressed the king so much that he gave them a position of great influence, which enabled Daniel in later years to guard the whole Jewish nation.

Daniel 2:28. Nebuchadnezzar, a heathen king, was given both a dream, and a vision by God. They showed him the future of the world, and his part in it. God also showed through this vision that He would judge all those rulers who stood against Him, by crushing them with a great stone which no one could avoid. Then God would introduce His great Kingdom which would never be destroyed.

2 Corinthians 12:1. Paul had visions of Heaven, and they changed his whole life and attitude. Although very few people are likely to see visions in quite the same way as Paul

10

did, we should not be afraid to ask God to show us at least something of Heaven's glory. After all, we are going to live there forever!

Dreams

Genesis 41:1–40. God spoke to Pharaoh in a dream, partly to show him a coming national crisis, then to show him that he would not be able to cope with it himself, and then to put Joseph in that strategic position which would enable God, through him, to save both Egypt and Israel.

Daniel 1:17. God did a similar thing to Nebuchadnezzar, and used Daniel as He used Joseph.

Joel 2:28. God did not stop giving dreams when the Bible was completed. Joel proves that they are for today as well.

Matthew 1:20. Joseph, the husband of Mary, not only had dreams, but he saw and heard from an angel during them. Although none of us are in such a special position as he was, surely we can expect similar things from God in our day. The need for them has not decreased.

False visions and dreams

Examples:

    Isaiah 30:10.
    Jeremiah 14:14.
    Jeremiah 23:32.

The fact that there are false visions and dreams, and indeed prophecies, does not alter the fact that there are true ones. Satan is not stupid enough to counterfeit things which do not exist.

Angelic messages

Angels do not have any power or inspiration of their own. They can only say what God tells them to say, and do what He tells them to do. Jesus said in Matthew 28:18, '*All power is given to Me...*'. Therefore power can only come from God and no one else. The great and undoubted power of

11

angels is derived from God. I believe that the Holy Spirit gives them the power they need to do the will of God among men, and He also inspires them to speak the word of God to people in a similar way in which He inspires us to prophesy. Where else does inspiration come from apart from God the Holy Spirit?

So then, when angels came and spoke to Gideon (Judges 6:12), Elijah (1 Kings 19:5), and Joseph (Matthew 1:20), they must have been prophesying.

Having said what prophecy is, let me briefly say what it is not.

It is not:

The only Gift of the Spirit.

Necessarily the most important.

A substitute for the earnest study of Scripture.

Most of the guidance God gives come through His written Word—the Bible. Many Christians are too lazy to seek God for guidance themselves, and will go to those with a prophetic gifting to find a quick answer to their need through a word of prophecy from that person.

It is not a reward for holiness.

Prophecy, in all its forms is a Gift from God. It is not a reward for those who pray a lot; nor for those who keep their lives clean and holy. It cannot be earned, but only received from God as He decides to give it. One thing to keep in mind though, is that, although God is King, and subject to no one, and although He does not need to give mankind anything, yet, in His love and grace He responds to those who, with an honest heart and humble persistence ask Him for supernatural Gifts of the Holy Spirit. We are told in 1 Corinthians 14:1 to *'**Earnestly** desire these Gifts, especially to prophesy.'* God honours those who do so.

It is not achievement, and it does not give us a high rank in the church.

No one can take credit when God uses them in prophecy. They cannot put it down to their years of Bible study or

Christian service. It is not something like a University degree. The fact that some may prophesy often, does not make them into a superior kind of Christian. It simply means that God has responded to their earnest seeking, and therefore uses them to bless the congregation.

The ability to prophesy is not a permanent ability.

It is a gift, given when the Holy Spirit decides to do so.

> ... *but one and the same Spirit works all these things distributing to each one individually just as He wills.*
> (1 Corinthians 12:11)

If we were able to prophesy whenever and wherever we wanted to do so, we would probably cause much damage to the Church, and become very proud too. God knows us too well to take too many risks with us.

2

There Is *TRUE* Prophecy Today

The gift of Prophecy has always been manifested in the Church throughout its history, even though it has been more evident at some times than others. It was in use when the Church was godly and pure, but it declined when sin was not properly dealt with, and discipline was not seen in the congregation. At other times Church leaders tried to control everything which was said and done by the people. This was a wrong use of their authority, and it resulted in the decline of manifestation of prophecy. Again, when Bible reading and prayer declined, the spiritual gifts were not evident to the same degree.

In these days, which I believe are close to the Great Day of Jesus' Coming, we are seeing a much greater manifestation of this Gift of the Spirit. There are many true and powerful prophetic words about, and they deeply influence, and greatly help the Church. Such prophecy is needed because there is great deception about as Satan tries to mobilise the world against the Son of God and His Church. But God is never taken by surprise, and He is raising up His own people to destroy the deceptions of the enemy. True prophecy is an important part of this Divine strategy. God did a similar thing in Bible times; it is logical that He should continue it in our day.

There is false prophecy about today

There was false prophecy mingled with the true in the early church. It is bound to be the same today, and we should not be surprised. However the possibility of the false does not rule out the reality of the true. In fact, it rather proves the reality of the true.

God exposed false prophecy and visions several times in Scripture. He hates it, and condemns it strongly because it misleads His beloved people. Several examples are given below.

> ...the prophets are prophesying falsehood in My name. I have neither sent them nor commanded them nor spoken to them; they are prophesying to you a false vision, divination, futility and the deception of their own minds.
> (Jeremiah 14:14)

> ...do not listen to the words of the prophets who are prophesying to you. They are leading you into futility; they speak a vision of their own imagination, not from the mouth of the Lord. (Jeremiah 23:16–22)

God warns us of it in our days too.

> Lord, did we not prophesy in your name?... He will say 'I never knew you'. (Matthew 7:22; 24:11)

> false prophets arose...just as false **teachers**. (2 Peter 2:1)

But God does not say that because there is false prophecy, we should not prophesy. Rather, He says that we should seek and speak out true prophecy. Truth is our defence against error.

Apart from the devil's false prophecy, there is a danger that some prophecies given by Christians can be harmful because it comes from their imagination and not from the

16

Lord. Some of God's ambitious people can even use prophecy as a way of making their voice heard in Church, so that they can direct its activities. Such people do a lot of harm.

Again I say that we must not discourage the prophetic gift because it can be dangerous. Remember that even preaching can be dangerous. Are we then to stop preaching?

Fear of prophecy can grieve the Spirit

Scripture is the final authority in all matters of faith. But direct revelation, either verbal or visual is part of the revelation of God to His people. The Bible contains all that we need in order to be saved, but it does not exhaust what God has in His heart for us. Think of the following verse:

> *Jesus said: I have many more things to say to you, but you cannot bear them now. But when He, the Spirit comes... whatever He hears He will speak.*
>
> (John 16:12–13)

The Spirit of God is telling us in our day some of the things which Jesus did not say when He was on earth. Surely some of those things come to us from Him by the spiritual gifts. Of course, God will not add 'new truth', but He will amplify what is written in the Bible.

Many Church leaders are afraid of prophecy because they reason that it can be misused, and that people could add to the Bible and introduce heresy. This can be a healthy fear, but if it goes too far and causes us to ignore or suppress these gifts, then the devil has triumphed, because he hates these gifts which expose his deceptions, and draw attention to the Son of God as His power is manifested through them in the Church. In addition the Spirit of God is grieved, and we are expressly told not to do this in Ephesians 4:30, '*And do not grieve the Holy Spirit of God...*'.

17

3

Objections To Prophecy

Love is important, not the Gifts

Some teachers say that love is the vital evidence of spiritual life. They use 1 Corinthians 13 as a proof of this. Therefore they teach that the spiritual gifts are not to be sought after today. They argue that the fruit of the Spirit is far more important than the evidences of the Spirit's power.

I wholeheartedly agree that love and the fruit of the Spirit are a vital necessity in the Christian's life and ministry. In fact the Bible says that if the gifts are manifested without love, then that manifestation is worthless (1 Corinthians 13:1–2). The life of the Lord Jesus was also characterised by love and the fruit of the Spirit. When Jesus prophesied, however strong that prophecy was, He always spoke it out with love and grace. But He did not only show love, He showed the power of the Spirit by manifesting the spiritual gifts too. It is not either or, but both and. In fact, if Jesus had only shown the love of God, He would have failed in His ministry, for, as Paul writes in Romans 1:6, '*the Gospel is not words (and character) only but the power of God...*'. Jesus showed the power of God by what He was, and what He said, and what He did or manifested, i.e., the confirming signs or gifts of the Spirit Who empowered Him to do so. The early disciples lived the life and preached the Gospel, but they needed the evidence that God was working with them, and in Mark 16:17 God promised them signs alongside their character and preaching. In verse 20 it plainly says that *'the Lord worked with them, and confirmed the word by the signs following.'* Prophecy is one of those signs.

There is no need for these gifts

Our main task is to preach the Gospel to those who have not heard it. We must not get diverted from that by anything. Some Christians have got so involved in pursuing the gifts and experiences of the Holy Spirit that they have no time left for preaching the Gospel. This can never be right, for it shows that their main interest is finding excitement and personal satisfaction rather than a desire to win the lost. The Spirit of God is not interested in sensationalism, and He does not give His Gifts in order to produce it, but to open the way for the Gospel or the health of the Church, depending in what context the prophecy is given. He is seeking all the time to focus our attention on the Son of God just as Jesus said He would in John 16:14, *'He will glorify Me...'*. And as part of this glorifying He shows the power of God through these sign gifts as we preach the Gospel in His Name.

If there is a need today for the healing of the sick, then, apart from the skill of the doctors, there is surely a need of Divine healing through the biblical gift of healings? If there are demon spirits possessing the minds and lives of people today, there is a need to uncover them through the gift of the discerning of spirits, so that we can deal with them in the power of God. Some of these evil spirits are deceiving spirits, some are unclean spirits, but whatever their characteristics, the revelatory gift of prophecy is essential in their unmasking and destruction. How then can we omit this gift and say that it is not necessary today? I say that there is a greater need for it than ever today.

These gifts ceased with Apostles, or Canon of Scripture

Many teachers say that prophecy and other gifts ceased with the Apostolic age, quoting 1 Corinthians 13:8–10, *'Love never fails; but if there are gifts of prophecy, they will cease... when the perfect comes, the partial will be done away.'* Some of them teach that 'the perfect' referred to here means the completed (perfect) Canon of Scripture. They say that because we now have the whole revelation from God, we no longer need these gifts such as prophecy, because the Bible has replaced spiritual gifts. This cannot be true. In fact, the completed (perfect) Bible still contains the exhortation to the church to *'Pursue love, yet desire earnestly spiritual gifts, especially that you may prophesy'* (1 Corinthians 14:1). It is wise to read the terrible warning in Revelation 22:18–19, *'... if any one adds to the prophecy of this book, God shall add to him the plagues... and if any one takes away from the prophecy of this book, God shall take away his part from the tree of life...'.* If God commands us to seek these gifts, we dare not say that they are not needed today. To do so would disobey the Scripture I have just quoted.

Manifesting the spiritual Gift of prophecy is not adding to or taking away from the Bible, it is speaking the word of God directly, but according to what is written in it. It must never be used as an alternative to it, but only to underline its principles.

Prophecy is dangerous

It certainly can be dangerous, because some who manifest the gift may be slack in their spiritual life; therefore the prophetic word could be affected by their lack of spiritual health. But are we to say that because a thing is dangerous we had better ignore it? If we say that, then we had better stop preachng for that can be dangerous if error is preached.

Teaching can be dangerous. The doctrine of baptism can be divisive and dangerous; so can the doctrine of communion. Shall we stop teaching these things? Of course not. Let us make sure that we are in the Spirit when we prophesy, or preach, or teach. Then we are safe.

Replaced now by teaching

Prophecy is not the same as teaching. Scripture clearly distinguishes between the two. Acts 13:1 mentions both prophets and teachers. 1 Corinthians 12:28 mentions both; so does Ephesians 4:11. Admittedly these verses refer to the *ministry* of Prophets and Teachers, but they will help to underline the difference between two gifts, and show that one cannot be mistaken for the other.

The argument that teaching has now replaced the gift of prophecy is quite unscriptural. The Bible shows that both are essential for the health of the Church. Teaching gives us a thorough knowledge of God's principles; prophecy reveals the specific purpose of God in a given situation. Teaching generally reveals the mind of God; prophecy often reveals His heart and His feelings. They are not mutually exclusive gifts, but complementary. Prophecy without teaching could lead us into error, or a dependence on experiences. Teaching without revelation can lead us into correct but lifeless formality. Perhaps prophecy is avoided by many teachers because it takes more faith and courage to prophesy than it does to teach.

4

Prophecy Is Necessary

Prophecy is needed today

If God gave us this gift of prophecy, and used it all through the centuries, and if He urged us in our day to seek and use it, then I personally say quite dogmatically that *it is* for today. I personally find it a great help and a blessing, and I teach it wherever I go. We should beware of those teaching schemes which seek to dispense with it. Dispensationalism (saying that the gifts were right for one period of history, but not for us today), is one of them. We must remember again the warnings in 1 Thessalonians 5:20: *'do not despise prophetic utterances,'* and Revelation 22:18–19 which I have already quoted.

Prophecy is necessary today, for these reasons.

To build up the church

> *...prophesies to men for edification* [building up and strengthening] *and exhortation and consolation.*
> (1 Corinthians 14:3)

To confirm the preaching of the Word

Mark 16:20.

To show that God is honouring and affirming what the disciples are preaching.

God urges us to seek for it and to manifest it

*Pursue love, **and** earnestly desire spiritual gifts.*
(1 Corinthians 14:1)

Scripture needs application

There is often a need to bring the specific personal or local direction into the general revelation of Scripture.

Prophecy makes heavenly things more real and exciting to us

When someone has a vision and they share it with us, it stirs our spirit and draws us closer to God. When God shows me visions of His great Throne, with all the angels surrounding it, and when I see all the wonderful activity there with angels going off on some errand for God, and when I hear the mighty songs of triumph and worship, it certainly excites me. Then, when I share it with the church, it moves our worship into a new dimension and often leads people to repent of sin. It seems to bring Heaven very near.

It builds up, exhorts, and encourages the Church

1 Corinthians 14:3.

If a prophecy describes the great armies of God in the

heavens and their constant successes, it nerves the Church for further warfare on the earth. If it describes the great mercy and understanding of the Father, it helps those who are discouraged to turn to Him and take hold of His hand and go on in their faith. If it describes God's wholehearted forgiveness, it causes those who feel that they have gone too far in sin to realise that they will never exhaust His grace, and they will come for cleansing and hold their heads up once more. Again, if the prophecy brings a warning from God or a correction, then they are able hear God's loving but firm voice and to respond or repent.

The major purpose of prophecy is to bring the living, personal word from God to those who need it, so that they press on in the great Christian life into which Jesus brought them through His death and resurrection from the dead.

Prophecy sometimes brings answers to prayer

2 Kings 19:20.

God heard the prayer of Hezekiah, and responded to him by sending Isaiah the prophet to answer his prayer. I know that we are referring primarily to the gift of Prophecy rather than the ministry of the prophet (Isaiah was a prophet, not just a man who prophesied sometimes), but we do not need to be prophets to prophesy, and I have had some of my own prayers answered by someone prophesying to me.

On occasions judgement comes through a prophecy

2 Samuel 12:1.

David sinned against God, and God sent Nathan to judge him through a short prophetic word *'you are the man'*. In my experience God has brought the word of judgement through a prophecy in which God described what He would do to a certain local church because of its sin.

Prophecy can bring warning

These warnings are not always related to judgement; they are sometimes given to safeguard people.

God warned Paul in Acts 21:10 about the treatment he would receive in Jerusalem through a prophecy from Agabus.

In Matthew 2:13 God warned Joseph through an angel who prophesied, to flee to Egypt for safety.

Prophecy expresses praise

1 Chronicles 25:3.

Prophecy is sometimes sung; indeed many of the Psalms are prophecy set to music. This is not the same as 'singing in the Spirit', which is a new language. Prophecy needs no interpretation for the words are understandable.

Prophecy mostly confirms

It generally confirms what God has already indicated to a person or church. It is a sort of divine underlining of the written Scriptures. This is one of God's ways of reassuring His people, and urging them on. Of course there are times when God brings something quite new to us through a prophecy, but that new thing will never contradict Scripture.

It is valuable in pastoral counselling

I believe in counselling, and we all need it on occasions. Some people need quite a bit of it when they are in times of crisis or special need, but we must be careful not to spend too much time on it. The main reason for counselling is simply to keep God's troops in good condition for the warfare. It is not to supply the need of constant comfort that some look for. The Church must be an army, not a collection of professional invalids.

Prophetic words are given by the Spirit; they often point out a person's real problem very quickly, and enable us to deal with the problem in a short time. The Holy Spirit, who gives us these prophetic revelations, always wants to direct our attention to Jesus; so we must be careful that we do not engage in so much counselling that we cause people to focus more on the problem being dealt with, rather than on Jesus who delivers them from it.

Prophecy, with its attendant gifts of the words of wisdom and knowledge is very economical. It can get to the root of a matter very quickly. It also tends to strip off the disguises by which people try to hide what is really in their heart. Someone described the gift of prophecy as a clear stream flowing down a mountain. On its journey it sometimes collects a twig, and then a leaf, so that there are several things flowing at the same time. Prophecy is sometimes accompanied by a word of wisdom, or a word of knowledge. At other times the gift of discerning of spirits comes into operation as well when we are counselling people. Because these gifts expose things as they really are in a person's life, often quite quickly, they release more time so that the pastor can get on with other things.

Prophecy in preaching

Prophecy in the pastor's preaching, can light up his sermons very well. It can add weight to them, and therefore tends to inspire the people's hearts rather than merely to inform their minds.

It often gives new direction to the church, though it can also confirm what God has already indicated in other ways.

Prophecy helps in evangelism

Prophecy is important when leading people to Christ in the first place. There is often a need today to uncover possible past involvement in the occult etc., before they surrender their lives to Jesus. Very often this uncovering will come about through the gift of prophecy. In many cases when I have led people to God I have prophesied to them, revealing what they have been doing that very day, and showing them what God feels about it. It has been a factor in their conversion. One young man was converted in the church where I was pastor because God stopped me from preaching and caused me to prophesy where he had been at 3pm that day; who he met with; where they went; and what they did. He cried out in fear, rushed to the front of the church and repented with all his heart and was soundly saved.

As I have said elsewhere in this book, the gift of discerning of spirits comes in here too, but these wonderful gifts overlap with each other. Often in the flow of a prophecy God will include a word of wisdom, or a word of knowledge, so we cannot compartmentalise the gifts too much.

Prophecy does many, many good things. No wonder God said, *'earnestly desire...especially to prophesy.'*. .

5

How And When And Where
Should We Prophesy?

Not all prophecy and revelation is given for public sharing. Some is given to help us in our private intercession. Sometimes when we are praying for our city God will show us things which are happening in it. It may be in a vision, or a dream; I have sometimes found myself, during prayer, speaking out things which are going on in the city where I live. This has helped me to pray more clearly. David the Psalmist often prophesied to himself, so it must be safe to do so.

However, most prophecy is given for public meetings. So, let us consider how we should prophesy within them.

Firstly, how do we know exactly *when* to do so?

First let me say that no one can prophesy at any time they choose. Prophecy is a gift, given from time to time by the Spirit as He chooses. It is not a permanent ability; if it were we could do a lot of harm by saying the right thing at the wrong time.

Some people say that they know when to speak because they feel a tingling sensation in their hands. Others say that they feel an increased heart beat. I believe we should be careful of paying too much attention to physical sensations. After all, if we sit on a nerve it can give us some funny feelings, but it is not necessarily the prelude to a prophecy! Nervousness can also bring certain physical symptoms!

The important thing is to learn to recognise the gentle urging of the Spirit within our spirit. We can learn to do this because He does 'speak' to us; this is shown in Romans 8:14, *'the Spirit witnesses with our spirit...'.* Because we are born again, we recognise our God's voice and Spirit. Sometimes we will experience a strong sense of God's presence with us, almost as if God is wanting us to stand by to speak for Him. Or, words will come to us and will not go away, so that we feel bound to do something about it. The Holy Spirit will never, ever compel us to speak; only evil spirits compel. 1 Corinthians 14:32 says *'the spirit of a prophet is subject to the prophet.'.* In other words, the one who has a prophecy which he or she could give, does not have to give it. The Holy Spirit has a lovely way of **URGING** us to prophesy, but He will never never force us to speak out. There are no easy ways to recognise the moment to prophesy, it only comes with experience. Faith is needed, and courage too. Most of us will feel afraid at times but we do not need to be afraid because the Holy Spirit is a gentleman! Remember that we are responsible to obey the prompting of the Spirit, but after that, the responsibility is on the church leaders to weigh and give an opinion.

We do not need to prophesy in a unusual voice; nor do we need to use the language of the old Bible. God expects us to use our normal voice, and our own vocabulary. Isaiah prophesied in one way as an educated man, but Amos prophesied like a farmer. The important thing was that God used them both and did not regard Isaiah as more important than Amos.

One important thing to remember when we prophesy is the need to speak up in a clear voice. There are people like me in every congregtion who do not hear well. What is the point in prophesying if the people cannot hear the word? One good way is to go to the front of the meeting and face the people. If there is a microphone, all the better.

How do church leaders handle prophecy?

Please remember that people who prophesy are usually sensitive souls; beware then of discouraging them. In fact, we may need to encourage the timid people who prophesy. Remember also that those who prophesy are bound to mingle their temperament with the way they prophesy, but then, so did Amos and Isaiah!

Make room for prophecy in meetings. The worship time is often an appropriate time for prophecy, or after the sermon. Expect it, and open the way for it. A prophecy may be God's way of changing your order of service, if so, let Him do it.

First make sure that everyone hears clearly what was said. Then, if the prophecy is important enough, let the leaders repeat what was said, then let them think about it and tell the people what they feel about it.

Leaders must learn to evaluate prophecies. It is very helpful if they sit near each other. If a prophecy is given, and the word has weight, a verdict needs to be given so that everyone knows what to do. If the prophecy is seriously wrong, give the verdict there and then. If it is not a very helpful word, or perhaps a general encouragement given more in the flesh than the Spirit, then leaders should speak privately afterwards to the person prophesying, but don't let it stop the meeting.

The best place in which to prophesy is within the church, wherever they gather, for it is there that the safeguards are meant to be applied. The Bible says, *'No prophecy is for private interpretation'* (2 Peter 1:20). So it must always be given where other people can hear it and judge it together. Beware of prophesying in corners; or of directing an individual's life by personal words spoken where others cannot hear what is said.

Some helpful ways of testing prophecy

True prophecy will be balanced

2 Chronicles 19:2–3. It will contain both warning, and approval.

It helps to have a few questions in our minds if we are leaders. As we listen to the prophetic word, let us test it by the following criteria.

1. Isaiah 8:20. Does it agree with Scripture?
2. 1 Corinthians 12:3. Does it exalt Jesus?
3. 1 Corinthians 14:3. Does it build up, etc?
4. 1 Corinthians 13:2. Is it given in love?
5. Romans 8:16. Does it witness with the spirit?
6. 1 Corinthians 14:32–33. Is it rightly timed and controlled?
7. 2 Corinthians 4:2. Is it spoken out of prior knowledge?
8. Romans 12:6. Are they speaking beyond their anointing?
9. Jeremiah 23:14. Does the persons life add up?
10. Deuteronomy 18:22. Is the word fulfilled?

Remember that some prophecy is long range prophecy! Some are not fulfilled for a long time, and parts of Daniel's, Jeremiah's and Zechariah's prophecies are still unfulfilled. But they will be.

Remember too that God changes His mind. Read the stories of Jonah 3:4, and 4:2, and of Hezekiah in Isaiah 38:1 and 5. See too the experience of Moses in Exodus 32:10 and 14. In these cases, prophecy was not fulfilled, but it was not because the prophecy was false, but because God, in His mercy, withheld judgement because people repented of their sin.

6

How Can We Improve
Our Prophesying?

There are different levels of prophecy, because there are
different levels of ability and maturity among God's people.
Different temperaments affect prophesying. Some people
are melancholic, tending to be very thoughtful, pessimistic,
and loners. Some are choleric; generally activists, quick
thinking, and impatient. There are several other temperaments, but I quote some just to point out that prophecy will
come in different ways from different people. This does not
mean that such people are more highly favoured than
others, but simply that God chooses to bring the stronger
words through them rather than others. There is a level of
prophecy in which someone will say, 'The Lord is with you'.

This is good and can be comforting, but there is a higher
level in which someone will bring clear guidance to a church
which needs it at that particular time. Yet another level is
that in which someone will prophesy in a way which brings
us into the very presence of God, and we simply bow down
before Him because it is so obviously a direct word from the
Throne. The one who brings such a word is not superior to
the one who brings the very simple word, he or she is just
prophesying on a higher level because God, and their spiritual training enables them to do so. Generally speaking,
those who have either the ability or the willingness to spend
much time in the presence of God bring the best prophecies,
whatever their temperament.

Preparation is important

There are no short cuts to effective prophecy, but this does not mean that new Christians cannot prophesy at all unless they undergo years of arduous training. God is very gracious and often allows a new Christian to bring a helpful prophecy to those who need it. But as these new Christians progress in their faith, and if they desire to prophesy stronger prophecies, God begins to make greater demands on them.

Importance of the Bible

Firstly God will require them to read, study, and memorise the Scriptures more than ever. All Christians must know the Bible thoroughly. If we love the Lord, we will love His Word, for the author is the one we love dearly.

If we obey the command in 2 Timothy 2:15, *'be diligent to present yourself approved unto God as a workman who does not need to be ashamed, handling accurately the word of truth,'* we will be better qualified to prophesy because our prophecies will be in line with Scripture, and therefore free from error.

The essential discipline of prayer

Prophecy is bringing words from the heart and mind of God. Therefore, those who bring them must learn to know God well, otherwise how can they speak in His name? It takes time and effort to know God, and, apart from feeding on His Word, it is vital that we speak often to Him in prayer. Prayer is one of the major disciplines for the Christian, but it is also a joyful sharing of hearts between God and His people. It must not be a grim daily duty, but a loving fellowship between those who love each other. The best prophecies come from those who practice what is written in Jeremiah 23:18: *'But who has stood in the council of the Lord, that he should see and hear His word? Who has given heed and listened?'* Notice that such a Christian 'sees' as well as 'hears'. In other words, visions often come during prayer times.

God's demand for purity

Those who would prophesy clearly and strongly must be constantly in the presence of the Lord. However, Scripture asks a very important question in Psalm 24:3–4: *'Who may ascend into the hill of the Lord? Who may stand in His holy place? He who has clean hands and a pure heart...'*. How can we spend a lot of time with a holy God if we are not clean enough to do so? God hates sin with a total hatred, and if we are hiding sin in our heart, He will see it and turn away from us until we have dealt with it. When we have done so, God will say to us 'now that you are clean, I can talk to you, and show you things which you can tell My people; because you have pleased Me by your obedience, we can work together.' Clean hands and pure hearts are essential for those who prophesy. If we respond to this Scripture, making sure that we avoid sin as far as ever we can, then we can come from God's holy presence with the clear prophetic word which will bless the church and urge it on to glory.

Courage and perseverance

Don't be discouraged by the high standard which God requires from those who prophesy. Remember that although He will not lower His standard, He understands us, and knows that we will make mistakes. Our blunders do not disqualify us from prophesying, as long as we are humble enough to learn from them, and to be corrected by God who generally does so through our leaders, or other people in the church who love us. Remember that God the Holy Spirit is with us, only too willing to help us and to lead us on. Take His outstretched hand, receive His help, and press on.

7

The Gift And The Ministry

Is someone who prophesies a prophet?

The Bible says that all can prophesy (1 Corinthians 14:31), though not all do, but only some were prophets (1 Corinthians 12:28–29). So, the fact that one can prophesy does not mean that they are necessarily a prophet. Prophesying is a gift; a prophet has a ministry. The gift of prophecy can be manifested by anyone who is filled with the Spirit, but the ministry of a prophet is given to him as a permanent ministry.

What is a prophet?

A prophet has a very important ministry
John MacLauchlan says, 'God declares that His activity will never exceed the prophetic revelation He gives (Amos 3:7). If we claim that God has spoken finally through the Incarnation of His Son, we answer that His Son is still speaking (Acts 1:1), and that He does this by giving prophets to His Church (Ephesians 4:11).

There are true prophets, and false prophets. There always have been, but we are considering the true prophets here.

There are no Bible writing prophets today. Such prophets ceased to exist when the Bible was completed. There will never again be need for such men.

I do not believe that we have national prophets today. There were national prophets in Israel in Bible times, but Israel was a theocracy; it was governed by God more than a king. Britain is not a theocracy, so we are not guided as a nation by prophets, although prophets may speak out within the nation. Prophets today speak mainly to or through the Church.

What sort of a man is he?

A prophet is a man who really knows God, and is very sensitive to His feelings. He is a man with a heavenly and eternal perspective, so that he looks beyond what he sees amongst God's people down here on earth and sees the Church's condition as God sees it. Then, he speaks out accordingly.

His personality is involved in his prophesying; so is his temperament, and background. He has been prepared from his mother's womb, and formed in the wilderness. (Explained later in the chapter.)

His burden is the will and kingdom of his God. His passion is the same as that of the Spirit; the expressing of the glory of Jesus in the Church, and in the earth.

He must be free from the desire to publicise his own ministry, or to get money, or form his own organisation so that he can have power and wrong influence in the churches.

Because his words can be so authoritative, he must remain humble and leave it to God alone to vindicate his words. He must not play the martyr when misunderstood.

What does he do?

He brings the clear, direct word straight from God to His church. A prophet sees (roeh, a seer), and he speaks ('nabi',

38

a spokesman). He sometimes sees something from God suddenly while in the church, and will speak immediately, at other times he will become aware of what God wants to say over a period of time, but will wait for the right occasion on which to speak it out. But he must be in an attitude of listening all the time, so that he is ready.

A prophet has a ministry, or shall we say, he is a ministry to the church. Ephesians 4:11 points this out. He is God's plumb-line for the Church. As he travels around the congregations God will show him what their real condition is like. If there is hidden sin in it, he will reveal it. If the leaders have a power complex, he will uncover it. If the church is in good condition, God will enable the prophet to commend them for it. God is very fair in His assessment, so must the prophet be. His ministry is often a painful ministry, and he is often thought of as an eccentric. Ezekiel was a prophet who was often regarded in this way, especially when he had to lie on one side for over a year, and be bound with ropes facing Jerusalem (Ezekiel 4:4–8). A prophet will not always be popular, for he will withstand all that hinders God's purposes. He is not afraid to wound, though his purpose is to heal.

So, his ministry can be summed up as follows:

He corrects God's people when they are wrong (Plumb-line).
He confirms and encourages them when they are right.
He brings them directions from God when they need guiding.
He reveals Heavenly realities, and the eternal future.

He does this through revelation, not because he knows the situation in the church.

Because his ministry is largely in the churches, the prophet must learn how to work with the leaders of the churches to which he is invited. He may bring the strong word of God to them, but it is the pastors and teachers who show how the church should respond to it in detail. It is not the job of the prophet to do this. The prophet must recognise that the local leaders have the authority there. He comes under that authority while he is with them. But he in turn needs to be received by church leaders. Prophets are not easy men to receive. But, just as they must come under local authority, and work with the leaders, they need encouraging, and co-operation too. If he is deprived of encouragement and oversight, he will become an individualist. If he is not received, his ministry will be denied its full potential. And the church will suffer because of the lack of wider input and vision.

Prophets must stay in good condition

In the magazine 'Prophets today' A.G. Gardiner is quoted as saying, 'The prophet is only useful so long as he is stoned as a public nuisance, calling us to repentance, disturbing our comfortable routines, breaking our respectable idols, and shattering our sacred customs.'

He can only do this if he remains close to God. This is true of anyone who serves the Lord, but a prophet is a man who must see very clearly, and hear very accurately, otherwise his ministry is useless. Even then he has a great need of the inspiring or anointing of the Holy Spirit to make his work effective. We can prophesy with all the right words, but if the power of the Spirit is not in it, the word does not affect the heart and cause us to change. It is likely that a prophet will prophesy more frequently and accurately than someone who simply brings a word of prophecy in church meetings, but, he, like those others who prophesy, still needs the anointing. In 2 Chronicles 24:20 it says, *'then the Spirit of God came on* (Heb. 'clothed, endued him with power to speak prophetically, or anointed him) *Zechariah . . . and he said...'*. If God had not given him the anointing or enabling, Zechariah could not have caused the people to change their behaviour.

Schools of the prophets

I believe that prophets are born rather than made, but they still need training. Some of these men experience much of their training in the wilderness. Such a man will experience deeper trials than others. He has a lot of grief in his life, he is many times rejected, and is usually somewhat lonely. Others do not experience such pain, and their life is more straight-forward. God uses prophets whatever their experience may have been, but He will ensure somehow that prophets become very dependent on Him, and quickly obedient to His command. Such men still need help from others, and fellowship with them, so, although we have Bible Colleges, we also need specialised colleges for prophets.

In Israel there seemed to be a sort of school of the prophets.

1 Samuel 10:5; 19:20 *'Samuel stood, and presided over the prophets.'*

2 Kings 2:3–5; 17:13.

Perhaps we could do with them today. For some years I have led schools of prophecy, which have helped those who want to improve their prophesying, and they have been most useful, but where does the prophet get his help, instruction, and fellowship from today? Where does his iron get sharp-ened as in Scripture? (Proverbs 27:17).

Are there any prophets today?

Yes. Ephesians 4:11–12 says that apostles, prophets, evangelists, and pastors and teachers are Christ's gifts to the Church. The Church exists today. God's gifts of pastors, teachers and evangelists are readily accepted by Christians today, why not the gifts of apostles and prophets? How can we split a verse in half, believing the part about some of the ministries, but not the other half of it?

We are in an era of unparalleled deception. I have been prophesying this since in 1972, and I feel it more strongly than ever now. God's remedy for it is largely, though not exclusively, prophetic revelation, *THROUGH PROPHETS*.

8

All True Prophecy Honours Jesus

If a prophecy draws attention to the one who speaks it, there is something wrong with the prophecy. As I said in chapter five, some people speak with a strange voice when they prophecy, others shout, some put a very unusual expression on their face while they speak. These things take away our attention from the Lord Jesus, so they cannot be right.

In every true prophecy we should hear words which express the love of God, and His grace and mercy. Even if the prophecy has some strong words from God, or even if it expresses His anger, we should still be able to hear the mercy of God in the word too. Sometimes God brings judgement through a prophecy, but if it is a true word there is always a way of escape in it. God will certainly do what He says unless we repent of the sin which brought the judgement in the first place. If we do not repent, He will bring judgement, but if we do repent He will not bring it. True prophecy will express this.

True prophecy will always say something worth listening to. I have heard many prophecies which are not worth listening to. Words which are silly such as this one 'Oh my children, I want you to know that I am your real buddy. I like to laze around on the beach with you because I made the sand on it.' God does not speak like that. It is a silly word. It does not honour Jesus or draw attention to Him.

God does not waste words. Therefore if some one gives a very long prophecy, it may not be of God at all, or, more

One of the best ways to prophesy in a way which honours Jesus, is to increase our meditation of Him through Scripture. The more we think through those verses which describe Him as a real person, the better we will know Him. Then when we prophesy we will be speaking on behalf of the One whom we know, and whose heart we understand.

❖ ❖ ❖ ❖